Need for Speed

Formula 1 Cars

by Bizzy Harris

Bullfrog
Books

Ideas for Parents and Teachers

Bullfrog Books let children practice reading informational text at the earliest reading levels. Repetition, familiar words, and photo labels support early readers.

Before Reading

- Discuss the cover photo. What does it tell them?

- Look at the picture glossary together. Read and discuss the words.

Read the Book

- "Walk" through the book and look at the photos. Let the child ask questions. Point out the photo labels.

- Read the book to the child, or have him or her read independently.

After Reading

- Prompt the child to think more. Ask: Formula 1 race cars need their tires changed during races. Why do you think this is?

Bullfrog Books are published by Jump!
5357 Penn Avenue South
Minneapolis, MN 55419
www.jumplibrary.com

Library of Congress Cataloging-in-Publication Data

Names: Harris, Bizzy, author.
Title: Formula 1 cars / by Bizzy Harris.
Description: Minneapolis, MN: Jump!, Inc., [2023]
Series: Need for speed | Includes index.
Audience: Ages 5–8.
Identifiers: LCCN 2021043624 (print)
LCCN 2021043625 (ebook)
ISBN 9781636906874 (hardcover)
ISBN 9781636906881 (paperback)
ISBN 9781636906898 (ebook)
Subjects: LCSH: Formula One automobiles—Juvenile literature. Automobiles, Racing—Juvenile literature.
Classification: LCC TL236.265 .H37 2023 (print)
LCC TL236.265 (ebook) | DDC 629.228/5—dc23
LC record available at
https://lccn.loc.gov/2021043624
LC ebook record available at
https://lccn.loc.gov/2021043625

Editor: Eliza Leahy
Designer: Emma Bersie

Photo Credits: cristiano barni/Shutterstock, cover, 8–9; Oskar SCHULER/Shutterstock, 1; Claire Slingerland/Shutterstock, 3; Darren Heath Photographer/Getty, 4, 6–7, 23tr; Nomapu/Dreamstime, 5; Nick Greening/Alamy, 10–11, 23br; ZRyzner/Shutterstock, 12; Mike Hayward/Alamy, 13, 23tl; Natursports/Dreamstime, 14–15; XPB Images Ltd/Alamy, 16; Buzz Pictures/Alamy, 17, 23bl; Cristiano Barni/Alamy, 18–19; DPPI Media/Alamy, 20–21; Natursports/Shutterstock, 22; Jeff Schultes/Shutterstock, 24.

Printed in the United States of America at Corporate Graphics in North Mankato, Minnesota.

Table of Contents

Speedy Cars

Formula 1 cars line up.

The race starts!

Cars drive laps around a track.

Zoom!

track ⟩ ····▶

cockpit

Each car has a cockpit.
The driver sits here.
There is no roof!

Each car has two wings.

One is in the back.

One is in the front.

They keep the car stable.

wing

wing

These cars are speedy.

They go four times faster than cars on a highway!

How?

Their engines are super strong!

engine

tire

Each car has
four tires.

They are wide.

Cars stop during the race.
Why?
They need new tires.

Pit crews change them.
It takes just two seconds!

The cars get back
on the track.

There is the finish line!

The flag waves.

We have a winner!

flag

finish line

Parts of a Formula 1 Car

A Formula 1 car's top speed is 223 miles (359 kilometers) per hour. Take a look at its parts!

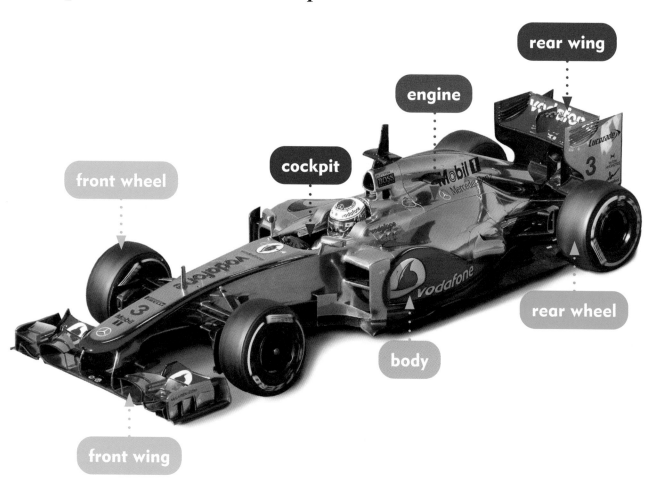

rear wing

engine

cockpit

front wheel

rear wheel

body

front wing

Picture Glossary

engines
Machines that make things move by using gasoline, steam, or another energy source.

laps
Complete trips around something, such as a track.

pit crews
Groups of people who fix cars during races.

stable
Steady and not easily moved.

Index

To Learn More

Finding more information is as easy as 1, 2, 3.

❶ Go to www.factsurfer.com

❷ Enter "Formula1cars" into the search box.

❸ Choose your book to see a list of websites.